D
I J K
P Q R
V W X
3 4 5
8 9 10

Featuring Jim Henson's Sesame Street Muppets

VOLUME 4

STARRING THE NUMBER 4 AND THE LETTER D

Children's Television Workshop / Funk & Wagnalls, Inc.

WRITTEN BY:

Linda Bove with
the National Theatre of the Deaf
Tony Geiss
Emily Perl Kingsley
Jeffrey Moss
Norman Stiles
Pat Tornborg
Daniel Wilcox

ILLUSTRATED BY:

Rick Brown
Tom Cooke
Mel Crawford
Robert Dennis
Mary Grace Eubank
Michael Frith
Joe Mathieu
Marc Nadel
Michael J. Smollin
Maggie Swanson

PHOTOGRAPHS BY:

Neil Selkirk
View-Master International Group

Published in the United States by Random House, Inc., New York, and simultaneously in Canada by Random House of Canada Limited, Toronto, in conjunction with the Children's Television Workshop. Distributed by Funk & Wagnalls, Inc., New York, N.Y.
Manufactured in the United States of America 0
ISBN: 0-8343-0052-4 (set); 0-8343-0056-7 (vol. 4)

4
Look!
I am in a dog sled.
I am cold but I am
happy...because I can
count the doggies
pulling my sled!
1...2...3...4!
Four doggies!
WOOF
J. Mathieu

Fun From Four to One
4
BOW WOW
3

2
YUM
1
That's what I call SUBTRACTION!

Winter

When winter comes, the trees are bare.
Snowflakes are flying everywhere.
The pond turns into solid ice,
Which Big Bird thinks is very nice.

With hats and earmuffs on our heads,
We ride down hills upon our sleds.
We don't care if the cold winds blow.
We love the winter ice and snow!

Roosevelt Franklin Washes His Dog

Here is Roosevelt Franklin
filling the tub with water.

Roosevelt is taking his
dog, Night Train, over to the tub.

Roosevelt is putting Night
Train into the tub.

Roosevelt is giving Night Train
a nice scrub.

There. See how
clean Night Train is!
And Roosevelt did it
ALL BY HIMSELF.
Good for you,
Roosevelt Franklin!

Cookie Monster

Home:	Behind the bakery on Sesame Street
Favorite Food:	Cookies
Favorite Cookies:	Chocolate chip, butterscotch, peanut butter, and macaroon
Best Friend:	The baker
Favorite Activities:	Baking cookies, playing "find the cookie," eating cookies
Favorite Stories:	"Goldilocks and the Three Cookies," "Snow White and the Seven Cookies," and "Little Red Riding Cookie"
Pet Peeve:	No more cookies
Favorite Wish:	More cookies
Favorite Sayings:	"Me want cookie!" and "Cowabunga!"

Who Stole the Count's Thunder?

The thing that the Count loved second-most—right after counting—was his thunder. Every time he counted something—whether it was bats, hats, or cats—lightning would flash and thunder would go BOOM! And he would laugh with joy.

Wherever the Count went, his own special thundercloud went with him. The cloud floated over his head and was always ready to flash and go "BOOM!"—whether it was night or day.

It boomed in the morning, when he counted sunbeams at sunrise.

It boomed at noon, when he counted people eating lunch at Mr. Hooper's store.

And at night in his castle, it boomed when he counted bats to help him fall asleep.

One morning the Count got up, opened the window, and took three deep breaths. "One, two, three beautiful breaths!" he counted. But there was *no thunder*!

Then he brushed his teeth and counted *them*—both of them—and there was no thunder!

The Count could not believe his pointed ears! He ran back to the window and looked up.

"Gadzooks!" he cried. "My cloud is gone. *Someone has stolen my thunder!*

"I will ask my friends on Sesame Street if they have seen my cloud," said the Count, and he ran out of his castle.

There was Mr. Hooper counting newspapers in front of his store. "One, two, three," said Mr. Hooper. "BOOM!" went the cloud, and lightning flashed. Mr. Hooper ran into his store.

"There you are, my cloud, my darling!" cried the Count, and he ran down Sesame Street, his cape flying behind him. But just as he got to Mr. Hooper's Store, the cloud sailed away. "Stop, thunder!" cried the Count. But the faster he ran, the faster the cloud floated away. Then it stopped and hung right over Big Bird, who was playing jacks.

"One, two, three jacks," counted Big Bird. "BOOM!" went the cloud. "Sounds like rain," said Big Bird. He opened his umbrella and kept on counting, "four, five, six."

The Count ran toward Big Bird, but the cloud sailed off again—and stopped right over a trash can where

Oscar the Grouch was counting his old shoe collection. "One scruffy old sneaker, two rotten old sneakers . . . heh, heh, heh!" "BOOM!" went the cloud . . . and it *disappeared*!

"My thunder is gone again!" said the Count, and he headed home. "One step, two steps," he counted sadly as he walked back toward his castle–and he began to cry. "One tear, two tears, three tears. And one sob," he counted. But there was no thunder.

When the Count reached the castle of his next-door neighbor, the Amazing Mumford, he decided to pay him a visit. Maybe the magician could help him get his cloud back!

Inside the castle he found Mumford knee-deep in rabbits. "A LA PEANUT-BUTTER SANDWICHES!" said Mumford, reaching in his hat and pulling out another bunny by the ears. "Seven hundred and twelve rabbits," he counted. "BOOM!" went the thunder.

The Count looked out the window and there, overhead, was his very own cloud!

"So, Mumford," said the Count, "it is *you* who stole my thunder!"

"Yes," said the magician, "it is I, the Amazing Mumford!"

"You are amazing but not amusing," said the Count. "Why did you steal my thunder?"

"Because every night I could hear you counting bats next door," answered Mumford. "BOOM, BOOM, BOOM! (The walls are so thin in these new castles.) The noise kept me awake. I was so tired I couldn't lift a hare. So I used magic trick

number ninety-two, the famous thunder-stealing trick, and I made sure your thunder would stay with people who count only in the daytime."

"But I *need* my thunder," said the Count. "If I don't count bats, I can't sleep."

"And if you *do* count bats," said Mumford, "*I* can't sleep."

"But I *must* have my thunder," pleaded the Count. "A day without thunder is like a night without wolves! Without my thunder I don't know when I've stopped counting. Without my thunder I don't know when to go 'Ah-haha!' I love my thunder! It makes me laugh. It makes me sing. It clears my sinuses. Besides, it's been in the family for a thousand years. You must get me my cloud back!"

"Wait!" said the Amazing Mumford. "I, the Amazing Mumford, have solved the problem! I will not only give you your cloud, I will give you *two* clouds! A LA PEANUT-BUTTER SANDWICHES!" he cried, and he waved his magic wand.

And—PRESTO!—over the Count's head appeared not one but *two* personal thunderclouds . . . a big noisy cloud for daytime counting, and a small quiet cloud to use at night!

The Count looked up. "One, *two* thunderclouds!" he cried happily.

"BOOM!" answered the big cloud.

"Ah-haha!" said the Count, getting the last laugh.

And from that day on, the Count had two kinds of thunder—loud thunder for counting in the daytime, and soft thunder for counting at night!

1.
Time for a Snack!
OR
GET IT WHILE IT'S THERE!
IT IS SNACK TIME! I, GROVER, AM GOING TO HELP WITH SNACK.
2.
FIRST, I PUT THE CUPS ON THE TABLE. ONE FOR EACH PERSON!
3.
THEN I PUT THE PLATES ON THE TABLE. ONE FOR EACH PERSON!
4.
?
NOW IT IS TIME TO POUR THE JUICE.
JUICE

5.
NOW IT IS TIME TO WIPE UP THE JUICE I SPILLED.
OH WELL. NOBODY IS PERFECT.
6.
NOW IT IS TIME TO PASS OUT THE YUMMY NUTS AND RAISINS.
RAISINS
NUTS
7.
NOW IT IS TIME TO TELL EVERYONE TO COME HAVE A SNACK!
8.
OH, NO!
YUM YUM
9.
NOW IT IS TIME TO START ALL OVER AGAIN....
THE END
J. Mathieu

FORMAS SHAPES
Say it in Spanish!
maggie

cuadro
square

rectángulo
rectangle

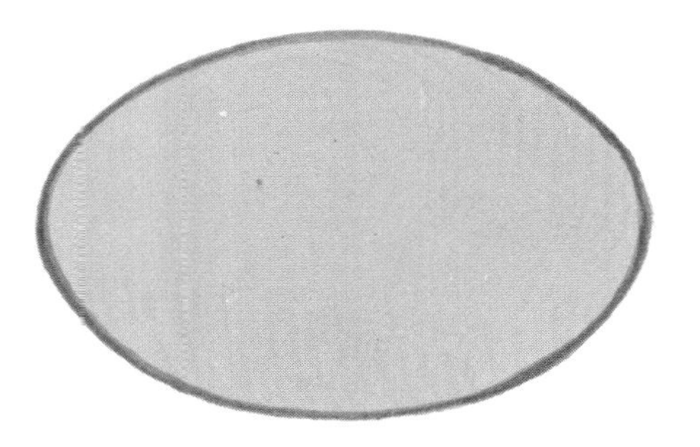

óvalo
oval

estrella
star

círculo
circle

triángulo
triangle

How Many Things That Begin with **D** Can You Find?

"Every day I walk our dog, Duncan," declared Grover's mommy. "And every day the same thing happens. Duncan doesn't dillydally. He decides where we go. He digs in the dirt. And when he's done, he heads for his dog dish. I don't think I'm walking him—I think *he's* walking *me*!"

School Days

school

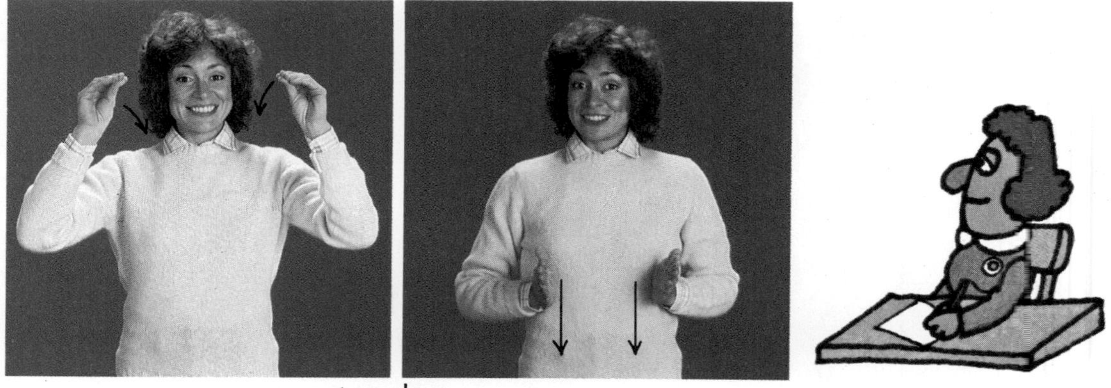

teacher

book

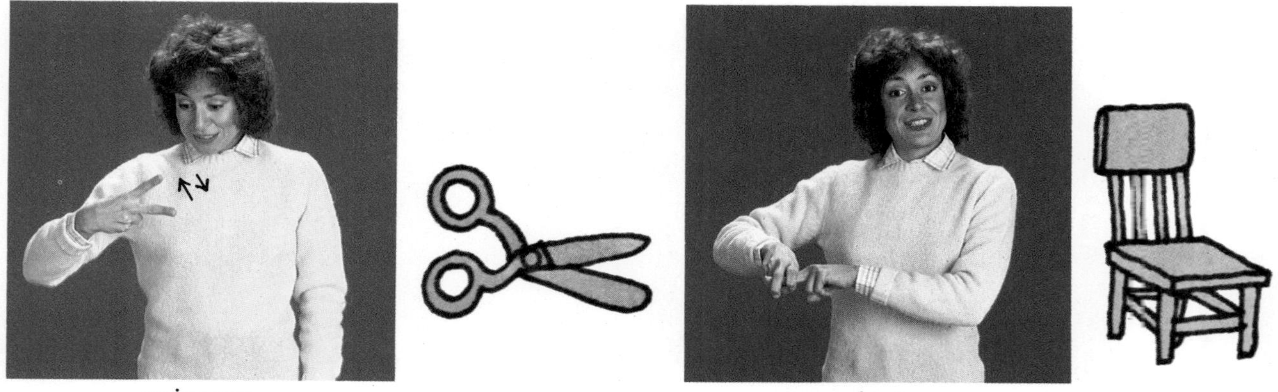

scissors

chair

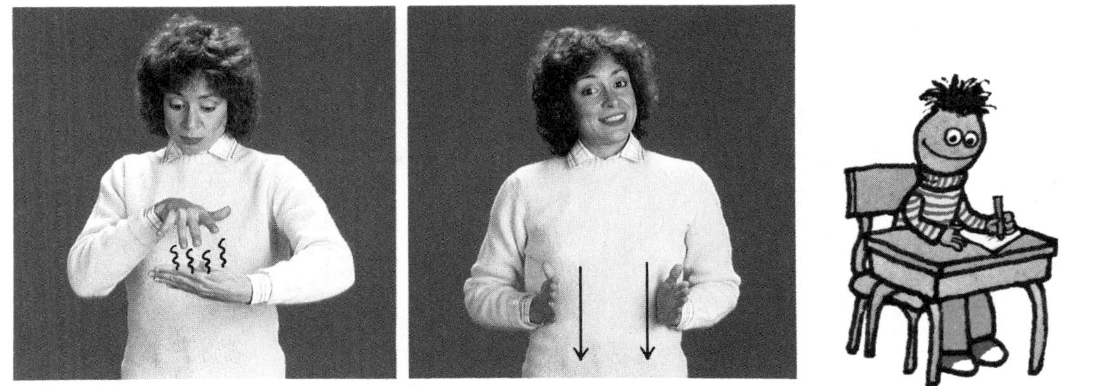

student

children

read

write

paint

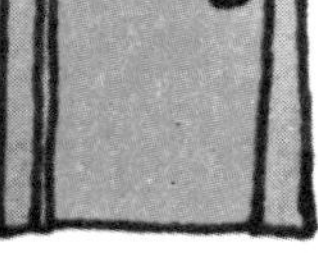

door

How many things in this picture can you "sign"?

I want to read

a book

about

cookies.

MANY
S
S
S
S

SEVERAL
S
FEW
ONE
Mike Smollin

4

Oscar and the Number Four

My name is Oscar the Grouch and my favorite number is the number **4**. Let me tell you **4** reasons why.

First of all, I like the number **4** because there are **4** wheels on a garbage truck. Count them. And I love garbage trucks because of all the wonderful yucchy trash inside!

I also like the number **4** because a skunk has **4** legs. Count them. A skunk makes a terrible smell that makes everybody run away. Heh-heh.

A table has **4** legs, too. And a table is a perfect thing to sit at when I eat my strawberry ice cream sundae with pickles and sardines on top!

And last of all, I like the number **4** because the page of a book has **4** corners. Count them. And after you count the corners, turn that page and then I won't have to look at you any more!! *Good-by!*

Oh, I love to take a bath
When I'm feeling kind of grubby.
I just grab my Rubber Duckie,
And I hop into the tubby.

But bathing does remind me
Of another kind of treat.
The bubbles make me hungry;
They look good enough to eat.

RUBBER DUCKIE FLOATS

The water makes me thirsty,
And my Duckie makes me think
Of a cool and frothy soda
That is both a food and drink.

So I'll fix a Rubber Duckie Float.
That's sure to quench my thirst
As it gurgles down my little throat!
But I'll finish washing first.

Rubber Duckie Floats

To serve two—

What you need:

1 pint of lemon sherbet
½ cup of crushed pineapple, drained (save the juice)
1 tablespoon of pineapple juice from the can
1 small bottle of ginger ale
2 whole pineapple rings

What you do:

Put 2 scoops of sherbet, the crushed pineapple, and 1 tablespoon of pineapple juice in a bowl. Mix them with an eggbeater. Pour the mixture into 2 tall soda glasses, and put 1 whole scoop of sherbet in each glass. Pour the ginger ale slowly into the glasses until the sodas become sudsy. Don't let the suds overflow. Hang a pineapple ring on each glass, and serve the floats with a straw and a spoon.

The Count's Counting Page

The Count is riding on a train!
His bags are on the floor.
And if you count his bags for him,
You see that he has **4**.
How many bags does the Count have?

The Count is riding on the train
With passengers that snore!
Oh, can you count the passengers?
You see that there are **4**.
How many snoring passengers are there?

"Your tickets, please!" Conductor yells.
His voice is like a roar!
The Count holds out his tickets, and
You see that he has **4**.
How many tickets does the Count have?

The Count is riding on a train!
He says, "I'll ride some more!
I'll ride and ride **1, 2, 3** times!
And then...I'll go for **4**."
How many rides will the Count take?

R. Brown

Big Bird's Story Hour
continued
O.K. I have chosen another story. But this time you must promise to sit quietly and let me tell the story.
You cannot blame me. That last story had piggies to count. I always count when I hear stories that have three little piggies in them.
FAIRY TALES
FAIRY TALES

Well, this story has absolutely no piggies! Is everybody ready? O.K., then. Here we go. This is the story of Goldilocks and the Three Bears.
Oh, boy, oh, boy! Goldilocks and the Three Bears! Wait! I must count them and make sure there are really three bears. Let's see...one...two... three! Yes, indeed... three bears!!
1 2 3
I thought you said you weren't going to count this time.
RUMBLE BOOM!
RIP!
CRUNCH
Pigs! I said I wouldn't count pigs! These are bears!! Ah, yes... one...two...three bears... three cute little brown fuzzy bears...
FAIRY TALES

No good, no good, no good, no good!
I can tell that this story will not work either. I am not going to tell this story if you are going to keep counting every time I mention the three bears.
That makes two stories you've ruined!
I'm going home for an umbrella.
FAIRY TALES
TWO ruined stories!
Count them.... One! Two!
Oh, it's WONDERFUL!
WONDERFUL!

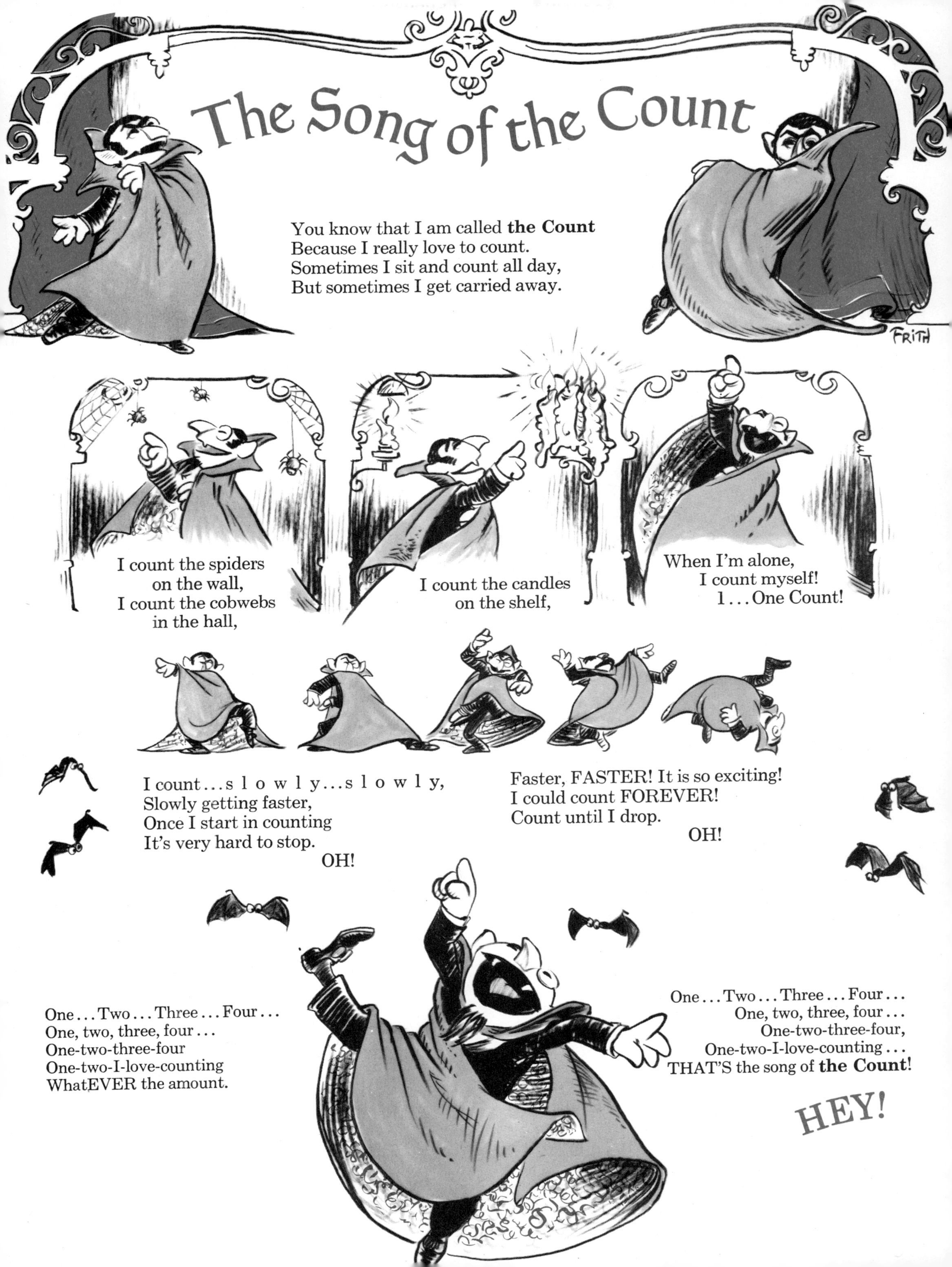
The Song of the Count
You know that I am called **the Count**
Because I really love to count.
Sometimes I sit and count all day,
But sometimes I get carried away.
FRITH
I count the spiders
on the wall,
I count the cobwebs
in the hall,
I count the candles
on the shelf,
When I'm alone,
I count myself!
1 . . . One Count!
I count . . . s l o w l y . . . s l o w l y,
Slowly getting faster,
Once I start in counting
It's very hard to stop.
OH!
Faster, FASTER! It is so exciting!
I could count FOREVER!
Count until I drop.
OH!
One . . . Two . . . Three . . . Four . . .
One, two, three, four . . .
One-two-three-four
One-two-I-love-counting
WhatEVER the amount.
One . . . Two . . . Three . . . Four . . .
One, two, three, four . . .
One-two-three-four,
One-two-I-love-counting . . .
THAT'S the song of **the Count**!
HEY!

The Case of the Missing Letter
I'm supposed to talk about the next letter— BUT IT'S MISSING! How will we ever know what it is?
Fear not, Ernest. I, Sherlock Hemlock, the world's greatest detective, will solve the mystery of the missing letter by looking for clues.
D IS FOR DONKEY
HEE HAW
HEE HAW
Look, Mr. Hemlock... donkeys!
Not now, Ernest. I'm looking for clues. Now, let's see. . . . The last letter was C.
QUACK
QUACK
QUACK
QUACK
QUACK
DUCK BEGINS WITH D
Mr. Hemlock . . . ducks!
Ernest, please. I must think. Maybe there is something in this room that begins with the missing letter?

D IS FOR DOGS, DINOSAURS, DEER, DOLPHINS
Mr. Hemlock . . . dogs, dinosaurs, deer, dolphins.
Ernest . . . close that door. I cannot look for clues to the missing letter with all these donkeys, ducks, dogs, dinosaurs, deer, and dolphins.
Aha! That's it!
What? Donkeys, ducks, dogs, dinosaurs, deer, and dolphins?
No, the **door**. Door starts with D, so D must be the missing letter. Sherlock Hemlock has done it again!
Dd IS FOR DOOR
Dynamite!
J. Mathieu

SING A SONG OF SIXPENCE

Sing a song of sixpence,
A pocket full of rye;
Four-and-twenty blackbirds
Baked in a pie!

When the pie was opened
The birds began to sing;
Wasn't that a dainty dish
To set before the King?

I really like learning sign language, Oscar, don't you?

In volume 5 you can learn the sign for one of my favorite words:
PIG!

A
B
C
F
G
H
L
M
N
O
S
T
U
Y
Z
1
2
6
7